BRILLIANT BUGS

CW01597342

By Matt Turner

Illustrated by Santiago Calle

HUNGRY TOMATO™

First published in 2020
by Hungry Tomato Ltd
F1, Old Bakery Studios
Blewetts Wharf, Malpas Road,
Truro, Cornwall, TR1 1QH, UK

Copyright © 2020 Hungry Tomato Ltd

No part of this publication may be reproduced, stored in a retrieval system, or transmitted in any form or by any means, electronic, mechanical, photocopying, recording, or otherwise, without the prior written permission of the copyright owner.

A CIP catalog record for this book is available from the British Library.

US Edition (Beetle Books)
ISBN 978 1 913077 198

UK Edition (Hungry Banana)
ISBN 978-1-910684-82-5

Printed and bound in China

Discover more at
www.mybeetlebooks.com
www.hungrytomato.com

CONTENTS

Extraordinary Insects

We humans may think we rule the planet, but actually the insects are in charge!

For a start, they outnumber us. At a rough guess there are ten quintillion (10,000,000,000,000,000,000) insects alive at any one time, made up of more than 900,000 species. And they're far older than us, going back nearly 400 million years, long before the dinosaur age. They're about 120 million years older than the flowering plants, too. In other words, flowering plants evolved to survive alongside existing insects, rather than the other way around.

Some insects live alone, but the more advanced—ants, bees, termites—form complex societies, working together to build megastructures, gather food, nurse their young, and defeat enemies.

This book looks at some of the most amazing adaptations of modern insects: their beauty, camouflage, engineering skills, senses, weapons, defenses, and sneaky survival tricks, plus some of the ways—both welcome and otherwise—they affect humanity. And the great thing about them is you have an insect zoo in your house and garden. Go take a look . . .

Great Survivors

A cockroach can live for weeks without its head. And the severed head can keep on waving its antennae for hours!

Cockroaches first appeared about 320 million years ago. Modern-day roaches developed about 200 million years ago and walked with the dinosaurs.

Cockroaches are scavengers. In a pinch they will eat just about anything: glue, grease, soap, wallpaper paste, leather, bookbindings, or even hair.

Some roaches are big. *Megaloblatta longipennis* boasts a 7-in (17.5-cm) wingspan; the Australian rhino cockroach can weigh well over 1 oz (33.5 g).

Cockroaches are fast! Once all six legs are in motion, a roach can sprint at speeds of up to 59 in (1.5 m) per second. And they're elusive, too, with the ability to "turn on a dime" while in full stride.

COCKROACHES

Flick on the kitchen light at night and you may see a flat brown insect racing over the floor to a dark hiding-place. Few insects are so unloved as the cockroach—but, of about 4,600 known species, only 30 or so are pests. Some are specially adapted for cold or dry habitats, but most are generalized, eat-anything, go-anywhere critters, which helps explain how roaches are found in almost every corner of the planet.

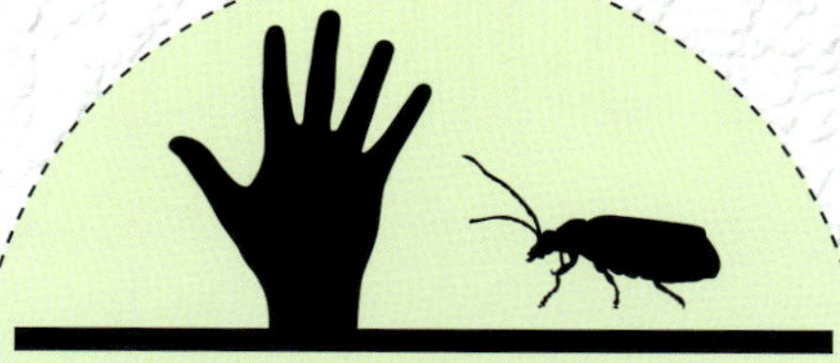

MADAGASCAR HISSING COCKROACH

GROMPHADORHINA PORTENTOSA

Size: up to 3 in. (76 mm)

Lifespan: 2–5 years.

NUCLEAR PROOF

In a nuclear attack, among the survivors would be fruit flies and cockroaches. They can handle mega-doses of radiation that would kill humans.

SWEET TOOTH

If a cockroach is introduced to a sweet taste, such as vanilla or peppermint, it will drool in anticipation when it later detects the scent in the air.

Working Together

Worker ants of all sizes cooperate. Left: An *Atta* major carries a leaf fragment, giving minors a ride; in return, they guard her from parasitic flies. Center: A *Pheidologeton* supermajor acts as a "troop transport" for minors. Right: An army worker grooms a soldier's jaws.

A weaver ant gently holds a larva and taps it with its antennae to make it release silk. The ant uses the silk to stick leaves together and build a colony home.

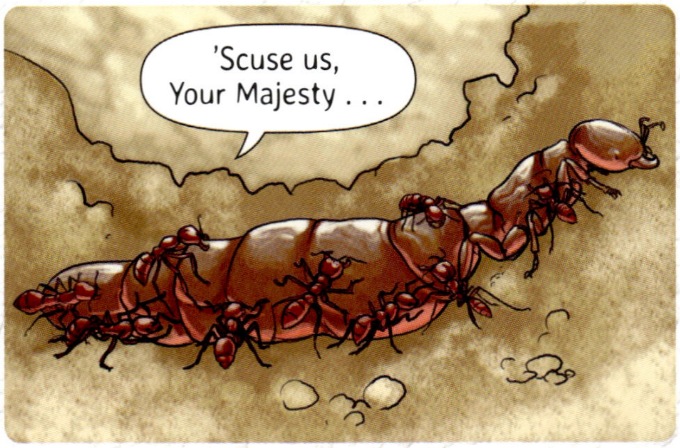

A queen driver ant is so big—up to 2 inches (5 cm) long—that her tiny workers, just one-tenth her size, have to push her around.

Some workers in carpenter ant colonies take defense to the limit. When attacked, they explode and die, blasting toxic gunk all over their enemies.

Honeypot ant workers, or repletes, hang from the ceiling of the nest and regurgitate liquid sugar and protein from their abdomen to feed the other ants.

ANTS

Ants are found worldwide, having evolved only about 130 million years ago from ancient wasps. They form colonies, sometimes millions strong, made up of several castes—queen, worker, soldier, and so on—all performing different roles. They work together to build the nest, raise the young, and fend off enemies. Ants will fight to the death for the colony's survival.

AUSTRALIAN BULLDOG ANT
MYRMECIA BREVINODA
Size: worker 0.6–1 in. (17–26 mm)
Lifespan: up to 2 years approx.

FIERCE

A bulldog ant is so fierce that, if it is cut in two, the head will still try to bite the abdomen, and the abdomen will sting the head.

HEAVY

If you took a giant set of scales to the Brazilian Amazon rainforest and put all the ants on one side, and all of the other land vertebrates (mammals, birds, reptiles, and amphibians) on the other, the ants would be four times heavier.

FEARSOME LARVAE

Antlions are holometabolous: they go through a complete egg–larva–pupa–adult life cycle. First, a female lacewing deposits eggs in dirt or sand.

The hatched larva digs a cone-shaped pit, burying itself at the bottom, but leaving its long, toothed jaws free. Then it lies in wait.

If prey tumbles in, the antlion may flick sand up to cause a 'sandslide', knocking the victim off its feet. Bursting out from its hiding-place, the antlion uses the hollow teeth of its jaws first to inject its victim with digestive venom, then to suck out the resulting 'soup', leaving nothing but an empty husk.

The larva pupates inside a round cocoon about the size of a chickpea. It may remain here, buried in sand for several years.

Finally, the long, slender, winged adult hatches from the pupa. It spends the next few weeks searching for a mate, and not feeding at all.

ANTLIONS

Antlions are not ants but lacewings, with about 2,000 species found worldwide. While the adult is a winged insect that looks like a rather scrawny dragonfly, the larva is a more fearsome beast. And while sometimes it simply hides among leaves or in rock cracks, it is best known for its habit of digging a sandpit, where it lurks with jaws gaping wide waiting to capture prey and suck it dry.

ANTLION

MYRMELEON SP.

Size: larva up to 0.6 in. (15 mm), adult up to 3.1 in. (80 mm)

Lifespan: larva 3 years or more, adult 25–45 days.

SNEAKY

The name antlion is centuries old. Maurus, a medieval scholar, said of the larva that "it conceals itself in dust and kills ants that carry provisions."

NICKNAM

Some people call antlions "doodlebugs." In *Tom Sawyer,* the classic tale by Mark Twain, Tom talks to a doodlebug to coax it out of its hole.

Borers and Battlers

These are male giraffe weevils (*Lasiorhynchus barbicornis*) from New Zealand. They look rather different from the Madagascar giraffe weevil opposite, but they probably fight the same "snout battles" to decide who mates with females. Their snouts measure up to half the male's total length of 3.25 inches (8 cm).

In the acorn weevil it's the female who has the longer snout. She uses it to bore a hole in an acorn, then turns around and lays an egg in it.

The larva develops inside the acorn, then drills its way out and drops into the soil, where it pupates for a year or two before becoming an adult.

The palm weevil lays up to 500 eggs at a time in coconut, date and oil palms. Its big larvae chew through the timber, ruining the crops.

Insects are rich in protein. In Malaysia, people cook weevils in a dish called Sago Delight. In Vietnam, weevils dipped in fish sauce are eaten alive. Mmm!

WEEVILS

Weevils are smallish beetles, usually with a long snout, and their antennae have an elbow joint. There are over 60,000 known species, and although farmers hate them because they burrow into plants and damage crops, weevils have some fascinating adaptations. In some species the snout—or rostrum—reaches extraordinary lengths, and males use theirs to battle each other over females.

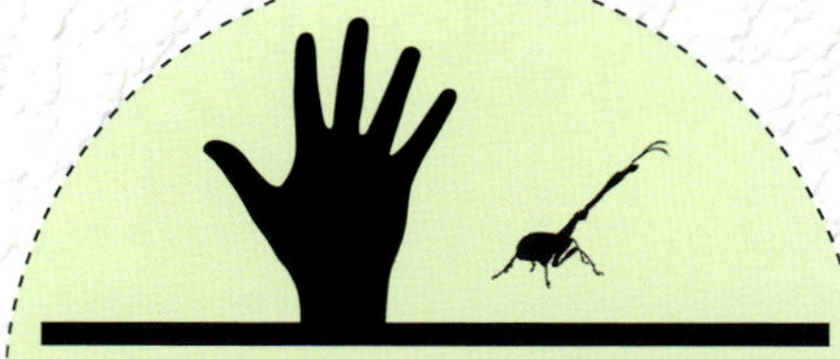

MADAGASCAR GIRAFFE WEEVIL

TRACHELOPHORUS GIRAFFA

Size: up to 1 in. (25 mm)

Lifespan: 1 year approx.

QUANTITY

Nearly one in four of all life forms is a beetle—and of these, around one in five is a weevil. Beetles are everywhere!

WELL-NAMED

The male Madagascar giraffe weevil is nearly all neck! After mating, the female (which has a much shorter neck) carefully lays her eggs in rolled-up leaves, one egg per leaf.

Incredible Hulks

Giant weta regularly weigh 1.25 ounces (35 g), more than a mouse. The heaviest on record—a pregnant female—tipped the scales at 2.5 ounces (70 g).

Like her cousins the crickets, the female weta has a spiked ovipositor, which she uses for laying eggs. She pushes the eggs into damp soil.

The mountain weta lives high above the snowline. It can survive being frozen stiff! It just thaws out in warmer weather . . . and carries on.

Tusked weta were discovered in 1970. Males use their tusks in jousting battles over females and rub them together to make a rasping noise.

Cave weta aren't giants, but they do have long legs, which may span up to 8.25 inches (21 cm) on a body just 1.4 inches (3.5 cm) long. You can find lots of them clinging to the roofs of cool, damp caves in New Zealand, so if you go looking for them, remember to check your coat collar afterwards! They're good at jumping too.

GIANT WETA

A flightless vegetarian with a face like a samurai warrior, armed with powerful jaws and spiky legs . . . and heavier than a sparrow? Meet the giant weta! All eleven species live in New Zealand, where rats, stoats and other introduced predators have wiped out their mainland populations, leaving the only survivors on islands or reserves. There are smaller weta species too, living in caves, forests, and even high mountains.

GIANT WETA

GENUS: *DEINACRIDA*
Size: up to 4 in. (10 cm)
Weight: up to 2.5 oz (70 g)
Lifespan: 2 years.

ISLAND GIANTS

Giant weta are examples of island gigantism: animals or plants that evolve in isolation on islands can, over time, become enormous.

UGLY

The Maori people of New Zealand named this insect *wetapunga,* after the god of ugly things, or *taipo*, meaning "ghost" or "spook."

Leaf Lookalikes

Antonio Pigafetta found leaf insects when he explored the Philippines in 1519–22. He thought they were "walking leaves" that fed on air.

Nymphs (young) shed their skin several times as they grow. If they lose a leg or antenna, they can regrow it—the limb gets bigger with each molt.

Phasmids have amazing night vision. With each molt, the eyes grow bigger but more sensitive. So while nymphs come out by day, adults are mostly nocturnal.

Some leaf insects spray a defensive fluid from glands in their neck to stop predators bothering them. If it gets in your eyes, it's very painful.

Relatives of the leaf insects include the two-striped walkingstick or "devil rider." The male and female are usually found attached together in summer and autumn when mating. They go everywhere together, and they don't separate until one of the pair dies and drops off!

LEAF INSECTS

The leaf insects, or walking leaves, have taken camouflage to the absolute limit, with bodies that have evolved to look exactly like real leaves. They have veins and ribs, and even crinkly brown edges. Related to stick insects, they are known as phasmids. Like some wasp species, leaf insect females can produce eggs without the help of a male, and the eggs hatch . . . into more females!

GIANT LEAF INSECT

PHYLLIUM GIGANTEUM

Size: up to 4.3 in. (11 cm)

Lifespan: 5–7 months.

RARE MALE

There are male leaf insects, but they're incredibly rare. The first male giant leaf insect was only discovered as late as 1994.

CANNIBAL

Leaf insects make great pets. But if they run out of leaves to eat, they'll eat other leaf insects instead . . . so you can't keep two together in one cage!

Cool Camouflage

The mantis is the only insect able to move its head through 180° each way. So it can perch stock-still and keep watching prey carefully.

The two dots that float around the eyes are false pupils: the part of each eye that absorbs light while the rest of the eye is reflecting it.

Like the leaf insects, mantises walk in a wobbly way. They do this for an extra camouflage effect, swaying like a twig in a breeze. The flower mantis on the left, however, is putting on a deimatic display—a startling move that shows off its bright colors. It sometimes does this to scare off predators.

Insect camouflage reaches beautiful extremes in species like the orchid mantises. They're hard to pick out from the flowers on which they lurk!

The mantis egg sac, or ootheca, looks like a squeeze of toothpaste, often fastened to a garden fence. Newly hatched nymphs look just like mini mantises.

MANTISES

The mantis is an ambush expert, a predator so well-camouflaged it melts into the scenery when perched on a plant. The big compound eyes watch for movement, and if another insect settles near, the mantis flicks out its long, spiked forelegs to snatch it. The many different species show wonderful variations of camouflage—some look like colorful flowers, others like rotten leaves or dry twigs.

VIOLIN MANTIS

GONGYLUS GONGYLODES

Size: female 4 in. (10 cm), male 3.1–3.5 in. (8–9 cm)

Lifespan: 1 year, sometimes 2.

THORNY

The violin mantis has an extra-long thorax, which resembles the slender neck of a fiddle. It also looks just like the dry twigs of rose bushes, where it likes to hide.

VANISHING ACT

A young mantis may change color—from brown to green, for exmple—when molting, in order to blend more closely with its environment.

Glowing in the Dark

A male *Photinus* firefly flashes a special pattern to attract a female of the same species, who then flashes a 'Come here!' answer that leads him to her.

Sometimes, a sneaky female from the genus *Photuris* tricks a *Photinus* male by flashing the correct answer . . . and then eats him when he finds her!

The New Zealand glowworm is the cave-dwelling larva of a fly. It lives in a 'sleeping bag' of mucus, slung from the roof on lines of silk. The larva spins silken threads up to 50 cm (20 in) long, covered with beads of sticky mucus. Then it 'switches on' the bioluminescent light at its back end . . .

Any flying insect that bumps into a dangling thread is instantly trapped by the mucus; now the glowworm larva reels it up and eats it.

In America, some beetle larvae glow to lure prey, such as millipedes. They are known as 'railroad worms' because they look like a train lit up at night.

Glowworms and FIREFLIES

Glowworms and fireflies can give out light, like a living torch. There are over 2,000 species: some shine to warn predators they taste bad, while others do it to attract a mate, or to lure prey. The natural light, or bioluminescence, comes from a chemical reaction in the abdomen. It's similar to what happens when you crack a glow-stick—except that the glowworm can keep doing it.

COMMON GLOWWORM
LAMPYRIS NOCTILUCA
Size: larva 0.1–1 in. (3–25 mm), adult 0.6–1.2 in. (15–30 mm)
Lifespan: larva 2–2 ½ years, adult 10–16 days.

EFFICIENT
Glowworm bioluminescence is a cold light. Almost 100 percent of the energy used is converted to light, with none wasted as heat.

LIGHT DISPLAY
Sometimes all the fireflies in one area will flash on and off at the same time, in a huge synchronized display. No one (except the fireflies) is quite sure why.

Beetle Defenses

The bombardier beetle mixes chemicals in its abdomen to blast out a shot of scalding hot poison, harming or even killing would-be predators.

Ladybirds ooze haemolymph from their limb joints, which not only tastes bad but also hardens on air contact, gluing up the jaws of attackers.

The palmetto tortoise beetle larva (*left*) hides in a tent made from strings of its own waste. The adult beetle (*center*) has big feet, each with 10,000 bristles and glands that can ooze a gluey oil. When threatened, it glues its feet to the floor (such as a leaf) and becomes impossible to dislodge (*right*).

If it crash-lands on water, the rove beetle *Stenus comma* skates away using "fart power." Gases released from special glands jet-propel it to a safe place.

Carrion beetles (and their larvae) feed on decaying animal carcasses—really dirty places! They give off ammonia to keep free of harmful bacteria.

BEETLES

There are more species of beetle than of any other animal group on Earth. Many are eaten as prey, turning up on the menu of birds, lizards, mammals, insects and spiders, so they've evolved an arsenal of spectacular defenses, including deadly poisons, explosions, cleaning fluids, and jet propulsion. Even the humble garden ladybird can squeeze out something nasty to defend itself!

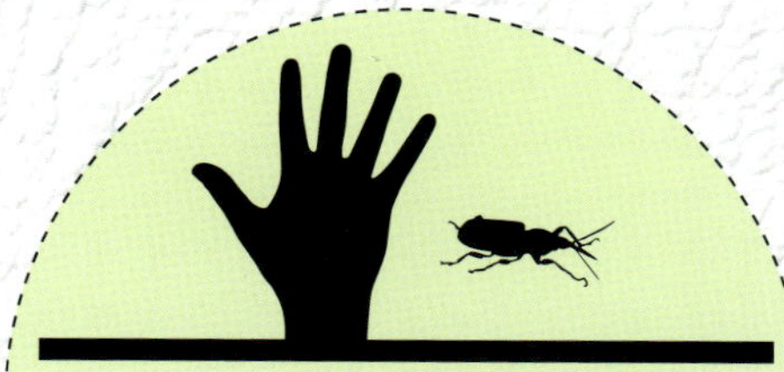

ROVE BEETLE

FAMILY: STAPHYLINIDAE

Size: <0.03–1.6 in. (<1–40 mm)

Lifespan: adult 20–60 days.

EVOLUTION

Chemical defenses of one kind or another have evolved more than 30 times during the 270-million-year history of beetles.

TOXIC

The haemolymph (blood) of some rove beetles contains pederin, a super-deadly toxin that is thought to deter predatory spiders.

Big Builders

Welcome to termite society! The queen, tended by a king, spends her long life laying eggs. Workers and soldiers are blind and cannot reproduce. Every so often, the queen produces some alates: these are winged termites that breed to start new colonies. In the picture above, can you work out who's who?

Termites are architects and farmers! Some termites build huge mud towers, complete with basements, air-conditioning ducts and fungus farms.

Soldiers defend the colony. Some have jaws, but this is a nasute: a soldier with a nozzle-like head for squirting toxic goo at ants and other enemies.

Drywood termites are a pest, living in our walls, chewing the timbers, and causing billions of dollars' worth of damage worldwide each year.

TERMITES

Termites are tiny social insects with a huge impact. Some species ruin houses and crops, but many others are the farmer's friend, improving the soil surrounding their massive colonies, which contain thousands, even millions of workers and soldiers, all slaving together in blind obedience to the queen (pictured below). And what a queen! Measuring up to 10 cm (4 in) long, she may live to be 50 years old—an insect record.

TERMITES

ORDER: ISOPTERA

Size: workers 0.15–0.6 in. (4–15 mm), queen up to 4 in. (100 mm) or more
Lifespan: workers and soldiers 1–2 years, queen up to 50 years.

MINI-COWS

Termites have been referred to as mini-cows because their multi-chambered gut can break down cellulose, the tough stuff in plants.

FOOD CHAIN

Winged termites provide more food for the mammals, birds, and amphibians of tropical forests than any other insect group.

Mega Wings

When a male butterfly courts a female, he hovers over her and showers her with perfume-like scents, which are called pheromones. This chemical courtship encourages her to mate with him. The male also chases away rival butterflies—and even birds!

Birdwing caterpillars taste bad! This is because they feed on toxic vines, and the poisons gradually build up in their body tissues, surviving right through to adulthood. They also have an *osmeterium*—a "stink organ" behind the head that helps ward off intruders like this possum (*above*).

A birdwing pupa, tied to a twig by a fine silken halter, looks just like a curled-up leaf. This brilliant disguise helps hide it from predators.

About the only predator that will tackle a birdwing is the *Nephila* orb weaver, a very large spider that doesn't mind the bad taste of the butterfly's toxins.

BIRDWING BUTTERFLIES

These beautiful butterflies belong to the swallowtail group. With their long wings and strong flight, they have been likened to birds—hence the name. They are also the biggest of all butterflies. Queen Alexandra's birdwing, found in Papua New Guinea, has the largest wingspan: nearly 10 in. (254 mm). Thanks to the toxins in their diet, birdwings are rarely troubled by predators.

CAIRNS BIRDWING

ORNITHOPTERA EUPHORION

Lifespan: up to 3 months

Size: body length 2.75 in. (70 mm), wingspan 5–6 in. (125–150 mm).

VIVID MALES

Rajah Brooke's birdwing is the national butterfly of Malaysia. Like other birdwings, the green-and-black male is more vividly marked than the female.

COLLECTING

There are strict laws on collecting birdwings, which are rare in the wild. Most species can be raised in captivity, though.

Humming and Hovering

The hummingbird beats its wings up to 70–80 times a second while hovering to feed from flowers, and gave its name to the hummingbird hawk moth.

The sphingids are big, strong-flying moths. They include the white-lined sphinx of North America (*right*), which also hovers like a hummingbird.

In 1862, Charles Darwin studied a huge orchid from Madagascar, and wondered what insect pollinated it. The moth (with mega proboscis) was found in 1903.

The hummingbird hawk moth is an impressive flier, able to side-slip while hovering in order to dodge predators, such as this praying mantis.

Some flies have an extra-long proboscis too. When similar features appear separately in unrelated animal groups, it's called *convergent* evolution.

HUMMINGBIRD HAWK MOTHS

If you spot a bulky moth hovering in mid-air next to flowers, collecting nectar with its very long, thread-like proboscis, it's probably one of several moths in the *Sphingidae* family that have evolved superb flight skills. They include the snowberry clearwing, or "flying lobster" of North America, and the hummingbird hawk moth of Europe and Asia. Listen closely and you may hear the wings gently hum.

HUMMINGBIRD HAWK MOTH
MACROGLOSSUM STELLATARUM
Lifespan: 7 months (including hibernation)
Size: wingspan 1.6–1.8 in. (40–45 mm).

HIBERNATION
In parts of its range, the hummingbird hawk moth hibernates, in a cosy nook in a tree or rock, from October until April.

REPRODUCTION
The female hummingbird hawk moth produces up to four batches of eggs in the year, laying them on bedstraw *(Galium)*, the caterpillars' food plant.

Life is Sweet

The queen (*center*) founds the hive, and lays up to 1,500 eggs a day. Fertile eggs hatch into workers (*right*), who forage for food, clean the hive, and nurse the young (far right). They also sting! Unfertilized eggs hatch into drones (*left*)—males, whose sole job is to fertilize the young queens who will eventually found new colonies.

Domesticated honeybees live in artificial hives, but their wild ancestors would have nested in tree holes and similar crannies.

In doing the figure-eight "waggle dance" for others in the hive, a bee shows them the direction from the sun to find a source of nectar, pollen or water.

Giant Asian cousins of the honeybee have a painful sting, but farmers welcome them because they pollinate crops such as cotton, mango, coconut, coffee, and pepper.

Bees are vital pollinators, but are threatened by overuse of pesticides and by Varroa, a parasitic mite that has spread fast recently.

HONEYBEES

As well as making yummy honey, bees pollinate one-third of all the crops we grow. These highly social insects live in a hive containing 50,000 or more workers and drones, ruled by a queen. Using wax squeezed from their body joints, they build combs made up of thousands of cells, where they store their collected pollen, honey, and other food and raise larvae.

WESTERN HONEYBEE

APIS MELLIFERA

Lifespan: workers 1–11 months, queen 2–5 years

Size: 0.4–0.8 in. (10–20 mm).

DANCERS

After returning from foraging, bees perform "waggle dances" and other moves, which tell members of the hive where to find food-rich flowers.

THERMOSTATS

By vibrating their flight muscles, bees can control the temperature inside the hive, keeping it constant, whatever the weather.

FUZZY AND BUZZY

The bumblebee is an important pollinator of early-flowering crops, such as apple. It gathers pollen in the fringed pollen baskets on its hind legs.

A single queen founds a new nest each spring, after overwintering. She builds the starter cells from wax, squeezed from her abdominal joints.

Compared to the orderly structure of a honeybee comb, the bumblebee nest is an untidy clump of cells built in a tangle of foliage or a hollow. The cells serve as honeypots, pollen stores, and brood chambers for larvae. Workers keep the nest tidy, removing any dead bees.

In the fall, gynes (young queens) mate with drones (males). The drones later die, and the gynes feed heavily, fattening up for their winter sleep.

A cuckoo bumblebee is a female that invades a nest, ejects the resident queen (*above*), then lays her own eggs, and gets the resident workers to care for them.

BUMBLEBEES

Fat and furry, the bumblebee is a welcome garden visitor because it pollinates wild plants as well as crops. Bumblebees are social, like honeybees, but form much smaller colonies, usually up to around 400 individuals. Unlike honeybees, bumblebees can fly in chilly weather, so they mostly live in cooler parts of the world. But this means their colonies usually die off in autumn, and young queens need to found new ones in spring.

BUFF-TAILED BUMBLEBEE

BOMBUS TERRESTRIS

Lifespan: worker 4–7 weeks, queen 1 year
Size: worker 0.5–0.75 in. (11–17 mm), queen 0.85–0.9 in. (20–22 mm).

WEIGHT

Aerodynamic "experts" once calculated that bumblebees were too heavy to fly! But they had forgotten that air behaves differently around small bees than it does around big airplanes.

DUMBLEDORE

One old name for the bumblebee is dumbledore. Harry Potter author JK Rowling used it for her Hogwarts headmaster, whom she imagined humming tunes to himself.

Expert Engineers

You can identify a paper wasp by its long hind legs, which trail during flight. By contrast, a common yellowjacket keeps its legs tidy.

Paper wasps often collect timber from old fence rails. Listen carefully and you'll hear a faint crunching as they bite it off.

Breeding males and females gather at a competition known as a lek, where males jostle for a high-up perch or fight. Looks are important too: females with the greatest number of black facial marks, and males with the neatest abdominal markings, are considered the most desirable mates.

Paper wasps prey on lots of different insects. In summer you may see them take caterpillars, as a source of protein for their own growing larvae.

The parasitic paper wasp *Polistes sulcifer* cannot build her own nest, so she takes over others and forces the workers feed her larvae—like the cuckoo bumblebee on page 34.

PAPER WASPS

First seen in the US around 1980, European paper wasps have since settled across the country—driving out native paper wasps and collecting insect prey to feed their young. The nest is a marvel of engineering: a bulbous cluster of open cells, usually suspended from a narrow waist or pedicle. Paper wasps often roam the garden in packs. Though less fierce than yellowjackets, they will sting if you get too close.

EUROPEAN PAPER WASP

POLISTES DOMINULA

Lifespan: queen up to several years, worker and drone 11 months

Size: 0.3–0.5 in. (8.5–13 mm).

NESTS

Paper wasps are named after their "paper" nest-building material, which is actually chewed-up timber and spit.

WATERPROOF

Paper wasp spit is amazingly waterproof, and scientists have copied its formula to create a special coating for unmanned aircraft.

Flying Aces

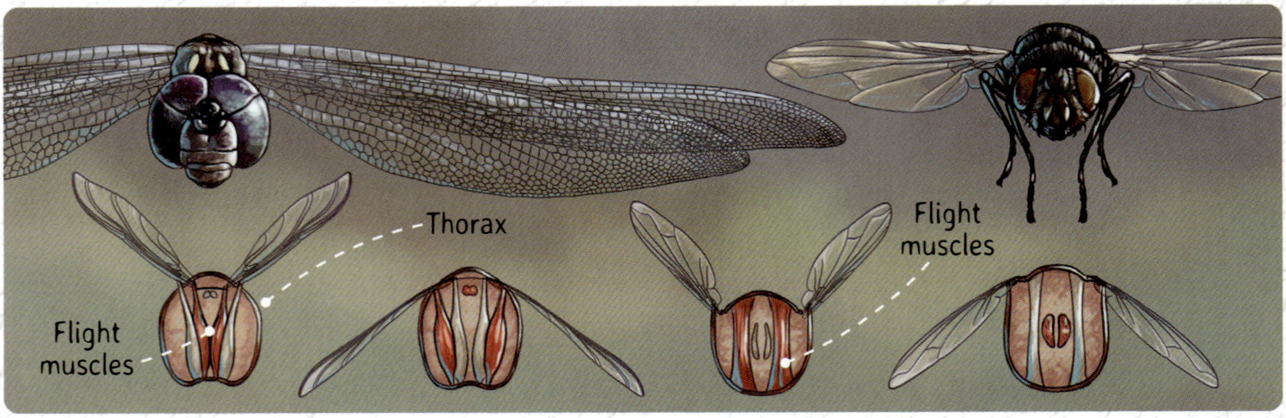

The dragonfly's wing arrangement (*left*) is primitive but powerful. At its root end, each of the four wings is attached to a flight muscle, for direct and independent control. A more modern insect, such as a housefly (*right*), uses indirect flight: it deforms its thorax to flex the flight muscles, as these cross-sections show.

The huge compound eyes typically meet at the top, for "wrap-around" eyesight. In some dragonflies the eyes are wide-set for better binocular vision.

The predatory larva lives up to two years on the pond bed. It shoots out its mask (a hinged lower lip) in less than 25 milliseconds to snatch prey.

Males are territorial, defending a patch of pond and chasing rivals away in aerial combat. The Australian emperor *Hemianax papuensis* uses motion camouflage, a special trick where he takes a flight path that makes him seem motionless to his rival, who can no longer pick him out from the background landscape.

DRAGONFLIES

Swooping and diving after their aerial insect prey, dragonflies are the supreme flying aces—thanks in part to their all-round eyesight, and also to the way the big flight muscles in their thorax attach directly to the base of each wing. Europe's biggest dragonfly, the emperor, can hunt non-stop for hours over lakes and rivers, especially when there's plenty of sunshine to warm its muscles.

EMPEROR DRAGONFLY

ANAX IMPERATOR

Lifespan: adult usually 4 weeks, but up to 8 ½ weeks
Size: body 2.5–3.3 in. (66–84 mm), wingspan average 4.1 in. (106 mm).

WINGSPAN

Along with damselflies, dragonflies form the order Odonata. Largest of them all is the giant helicopter damselfly of Central America, with a 7.5-in. (191-mm) wingspan.

DIRECTIONS

A dragonfly can fly in any direction and even upside down when chasing prey or rivals. But due to the set-up of its forelegs, it cannot walk.

Lightning Fast

The halteres, which vibrate during flight, detect any changes in the fly's pitch, roll, and yaw movements (up-and-down and side-to-side). They send signals to the nerve tissues in the thorax, enabling the flight muscles to constantly stabilize the fly's body. (If you want to see halteres, crane flies have a big pair.)

When you try to swat a fly, it calculates the angle of the approaching threat and within 0.01 seconds it has adjusted its legs to spring off in a safe direction.

Blowflies are often the first flies to lay eggs on a carcass, because their maggots eat rotten meat. Police experts look for blowflies on a corpse to calculate when it died.

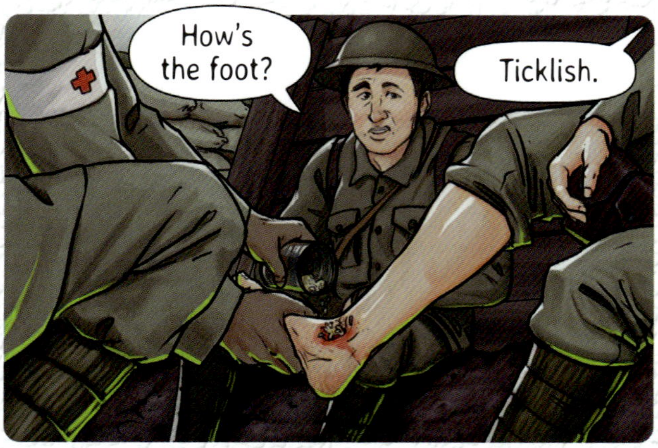

Because maggots only eat dead flesh and not healthy tissue, they have been used to clean up festering wounds—on soldiers in wartime, for example.

Scientists are researching natural chemicals in blowfly maggots. This may lead to new drugs to fight resistant infections or even cancer.

BLOWFLIES

So how does a fly fly? In the true flies (order Diptera), the secret lies partly in the halteres. You can read opposite to learn how these clever gizmos work. Blowflies, meanwhile, are those metallic-looking pests that perch on fresh roadkill or on a juicy steak in the kitchen, laying their eggs and spreading disease. Their larvae—the classic horror-movie maggots—have some uses in medicine that may surprise you.

BLUEBOTTLE

CALLIPHORA VOMITORIA

Lifespan: adult usually up to 1 month; longer if it survives hibernation

Size: 0.4–0.6 in. (10–14 mm).

EVOLUTION

A fly flies only with its forewings. Long ago the hindwings evolved into halteres, a pair of knob-tipped stalks attached to the thorax.

REFLEXES

Why are flies so hard to swat? Partly because of their all-round vision, also because they think much quicker than we move!

Swooping Hunters

Robber flies usually hunt on sunny days. They tend to perch in wait on a plant, then zoom off and attack in flight using their excellent vision and superb flying skills to zero in on the flight path of their prey. Spines on their strong legs help them grab the victim—and they always choose prey small enough to grab quite easily.

Many robber flies have evolved a warning coloring and appearance that helps them evade predators. For example, this fly (*left*) looks just like a bee (*right*).

The mystax is a "mustache" of bristles above the robber fly's mouthparts that protects its eyes from struggling prey.

The fly injects toxic saliva to paralyze the prey and soften its guts, which it then sucks up. The strong proboscis of a big robber fly can punch through a beetle's wingcases.

In one group of robber flies, the male has extraordinary hind-leg plumes, perhaps to impress a female during his courtship dance.

ROBBER FLIES

Not all flies feed on sugar, poo, and rotting meat . . . The Asilidae are a worldwide family of more than 7,000 species of robber fly: fast, powerful, day-flying predators equipped with stout legs, specialized in intercepting insect prey on the wing and stabbing it with their needle-sharp proboscis. This injects saliva that paralyzes the victim and dissolves its guts. Not for nothing are they also called assassin flies.

ROBBER FLIES
FAMILY: ASILIDAE
Lifespan: 1 year, maybe 2
Size: 0.15–3.1 in. (3–80 mm).

PEST CONTROL

Preying on ants, beetles, wasps, flies, grasshoppers, bugs—anything, in fact, that moves—robber flies are useful controllers of insect pests.

BIRD FOOD

Big robber flies like the bee panther *(Promachus rufipes)* or beelzebub bee-eater *(Mallophora leschenaulti)* have been known to attack hummingbirds.

FRAIL BUT DEADLY

A female mosquito can locate a host by sight, but is also attracted by smells—such as sweat and exhaled breath—from as much as 164 feet (50 m) away.

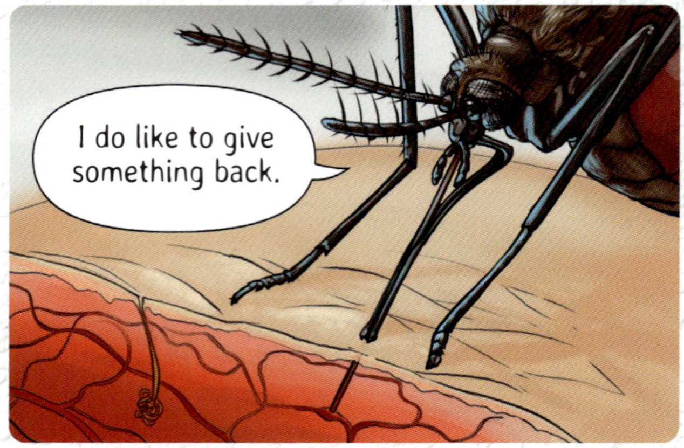

A feeding female injects saliva that stops a host's blood clotting and keeps her proboscis from clogging. It's when the saliva is infected that she can spread disease.

A male's bushy antennae can hear the special whine of an unmated female's wingbeat. If they are pairable, the two mosquitoes will "harmonize," like two people who begin to hum the same tune, and then track each other down. It's a bit like having a built-in "find my mate" app!

Scientists took many years to realize mosquitoes spread disease. Medical pioneer Patrick Manson (1844–1922) tested malarial mosquitoes on his gardener, Hin Lo.

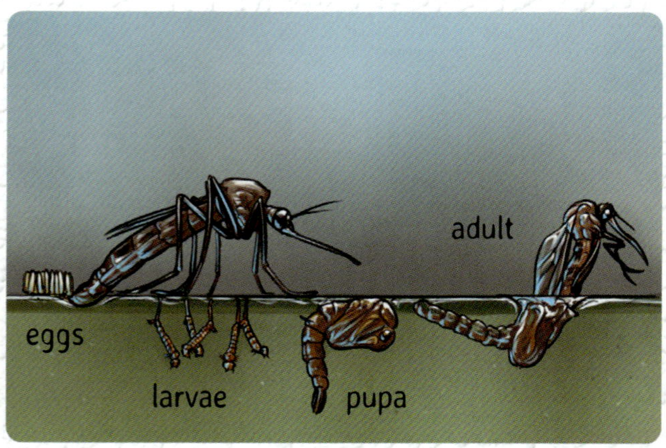

Most mosquito larvae develop in water, breathing at the surface and feeding on tiny particles. They also pupate and hatch at the surface—then fly off to find a mate.

MOSQUITOES

These flimsy little flies are parasites, the female sucking a host's blood to nourish the eggs in her abdomen. Some species also pass on diseases that kill at least two million people every year, making the mosquito the world's deadliest animal. And mosquitoes are terribly good at what they do: more sensitive to sound than any other insect, they create that awful whining noise just to find a mate.

MOSQUITO

FAMILY: CULICIDAE

Lifespan: a few days to 1 month or more

Size: body 0.1–0.7 in. (2–19 mm), average 0.15–0.25 in. (3–6 mm).

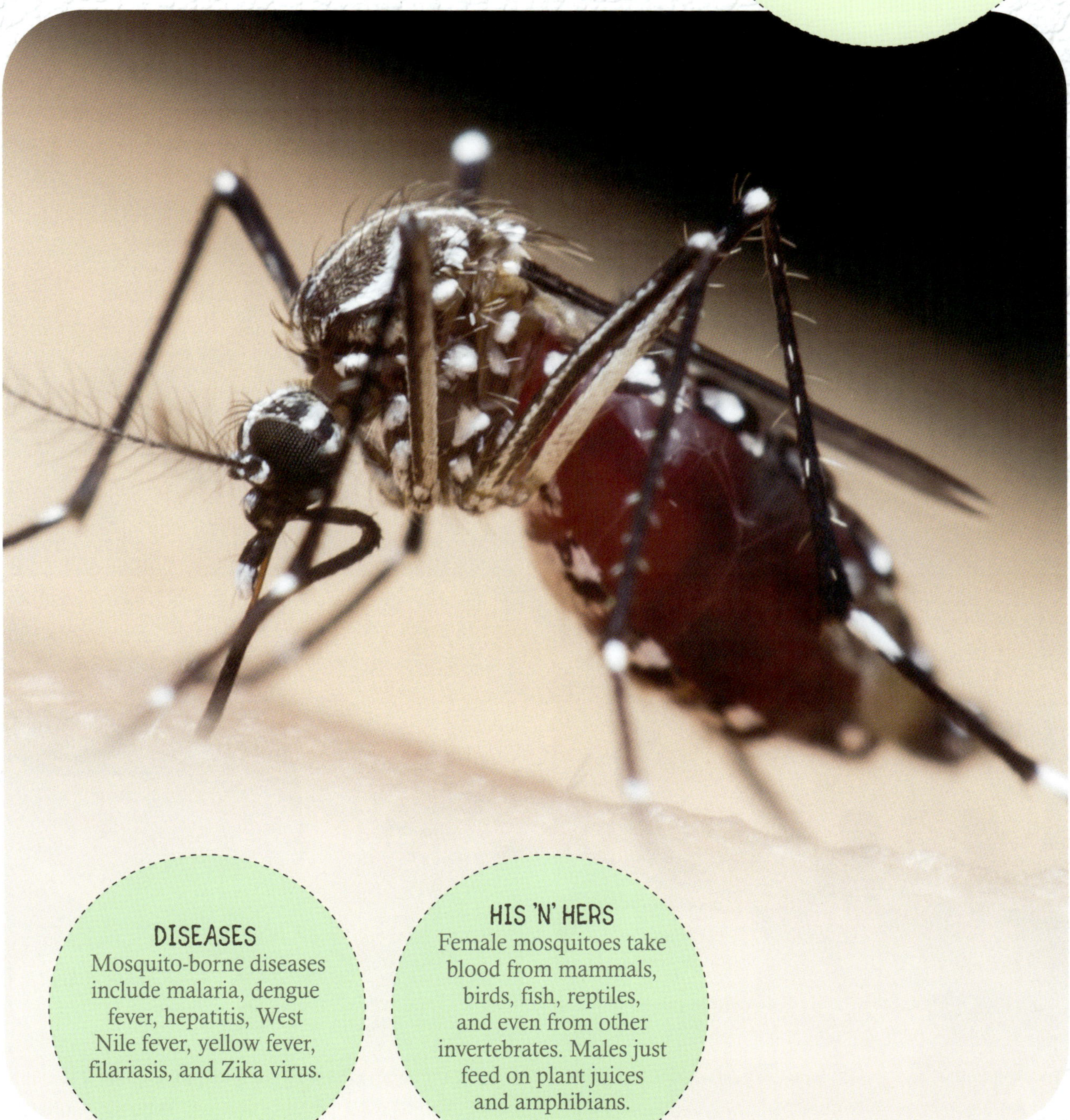

DISEASES

Mosquito-borne diseases include malaria, dengue fever, hepatitis, West Nile fever, yellow fever, filariasis, and Zika virus.

HIS 'N' HERS

Female mosquitoes take blood from mammals, birds, fish, reptiles, and even from other invertebrates. Males just feed on plant juices and amphibians.

Insect Athletes

To jump, a grasshopper contracts two muscles in each hind-leg femur (the thick upper section) so that they pull against each other, storing lots of strain energy. Then, by suddenly relaxing one femur muscle, the energy is released and the tibia (thin lower section) can kick down to fling the insect skywards.

To attract a mate, a grasshopper makes a chirping sound, called stridulation, by moving its hind legs, rubbing them against notches on its wing veins.

Some grasshoppers are brightly colored to warn birds they are bad to eat. Others (*above*) will suddenly open patterned wings to surprise predators and buy time to escape.

Environmental changes can trigger grasshoppers to gather and migrate in huge swarms of nymphs (young) and adults, devastating crops and even causing local famine.

Colorful grasshoppers are usually toxic, but the edible species are full of protein. Worldwide, around 1,400 insect species are included in the human diet.

SHORTHORN GRASSHOPPERS

Shorthorn grasshoppers don't really have horns; they have short antennae, unlike their cousins the katydids or bush crickets (with long antennae). The 10,000-odd species include the infamous locusts, which may form swarms many millions strong and strip a crop field bare in a few hours. While they can fly perfectly well, grasshoppers are far better known for their athletic leaping skills.

SHORTHORN GRASSHOPPER
SUBORDER: CAELIFERA
Lifespan: adult 7–8 weeks
Size: body up to 6 in. (150 mm), average 1.5–2 in. (38–50 mm).

GREEDY

It's estimated that, in a single day, a one-ton locust swarm can eat as much cereal as 2,500 people. In the Bible, a plague of locusts devoured Egypt's crops.

CATAPULTS

A grasshopper's hind legs are basically a pair of catapults, designed to produce leaping energy that is both rapid and powerful.

Tough Critters

Tardigrade means "slow walker." Tardigrades use hydraulics (body fluid pressure) to bend their legs, which are tipped with sharp, curving claws.

When there's no water, tardigrades dry out. In this state they are called "tuns," and a sugar called trehalose replaces water in the body to preserve the cells.

Tuns usually survive drying out. They and their eggs may be carried on the wind to new places, to start new populations once they're moistened again.

In boiling and freezing tests, tardigrades have survived temperatures from −458°F to 300°Fahrenheit (−272° to 149°C) . . . way beyond human endurance!

In 2007, the European Space Agency sent tuns and eggs up on a rocket to expose them to the vacuum of space. They were also exposed to levels of solar radiation that would kill humans. After returning to Earth 10 days later and being rehydrated, two-thirds of the tuns survived the trip unharmed.

TARDIGRADES

The tiny tardigrade, or water bear, clambers through damp plants, eating tinier animals or algae with its pump-action snout. And it's the toughest animal ever! In tests it has survived being boiled, frozen, pressurized, oxygen-starved, and blitzed with radiation. But its best trick, used when there's no water, is to go into a tun state, where it shrivels like a dry sponge and simply waits—for years, sometimes—to be wet again.

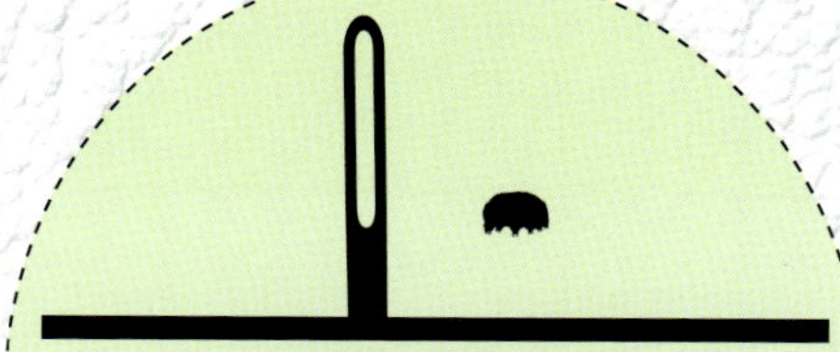

TARDIGRADES
PHYLUM: TARDIGRADA
Lifespan: 10 years or more
Size: 0.004–0.06 in. (0.1–1.5 mm).

PUFFED UP
When starved of oxygen, tardigrades swell up (as shown above) until oxygen levels return to normal. This puffy state is called anoxybiosis.

ALIENS
People have suggested tardigrades might be aliens from another planet. But as they can go without oxygen for only a few days, this isn't likely.

SURVIVORS
Tardigrades can survive pressure almost six times greater than that found in the deepest ocean trenches.

Ancient Killers

The velvet worm group—the Onychophora—is very, very old. Fossil ancestors have been found that are half a billion years old.

Flanking the mouth of the velvet worm are two moveable turrets known as oral papillae. These face-guns squirt jets of slime up to 12 inches (30 cm).

Velvet worms eat woodlice, spiders, crickets, and more. After sneaking quietly up on prey, a velvet worm slimes it to prevent escape. Then it uses the blade-like teeth in its powerful jaws to chomp a hole in the body. Finally, it injects the victim with saliva, which turns the guts to a goo it can suck up.

Velvet worms don't have a tough outer skeleton, but a soft covering called the cuticula. To grow, they shed the cuticula every couple of weeks or so.

Some species lay eggs. In others, after a pregnancy of up to 15 months, a female gives birth to live young that can already look after themselves.

VELVET WORMS

Squashy, leggy, and fuzzy to the touch, the velvet worm is not a worm, but a member of an ancient group of deadly predators. Living in damp leaf litter, it stalks a victim in total darkness, tapping it softly with its antennae to see if it's worth attacking. Then—splat!—the velvet worm shoots twin jets of slime from its face-guns, leaving the victim helpless to defend itself.

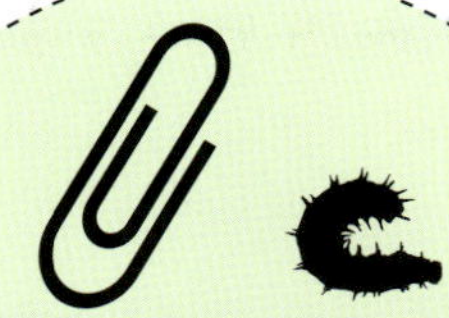

PERIPATUS

PHYLUM: ONYCHOPHORA

Lifespan: up to 6 years

Size: 0.6–6 in. (15–150 mm).

LOTS OF LEGS

Depending on species (about 180 worldwide), velvet worms have between 13 and 43 leg pairs, with claws that extend for extra grip on rough ground.

DARK DWELLERS

Velvet worms like darkness partly because they need to be damp, so they do not dry out. But if they get too wet, they drown.

HIERARCHY

Sometimes several velvet worms gather at a feed—but there's a strict pecking order as to who eats first, starting with the bossiest female.

Tiny Tanks

Whenever possible, woodlice squeeze their flattened bodies into tight spaces. One desert-dweller stays cool by digging a hole for itself, its partner, and its young.

The sea slater *Ligia oceanica*, a cousin of the woodlice, lives in the splash zone on the beach. It breathes air, hides in damp cracks, and eats decaying seaweed.

Woodlice of the family *Armadillidae* are known as pillbugs or roly-polies. They can curl their body up like a tiny armadillo when threatened by danger. You can find them in the garden. Their body is more rounded than a woodlouse's, but they're easily confused with pill millipedes, which are completely different animals.

Babies, known as mancas, hatch in a pouch on the mother's underside. A common pillbug (*left*) curls up to release her mancas; while a sea slater (*right*) raises her abdomen.

A distant cousin of woodlice is the giant isopod, *Bathynomus giganteus*, which can reach a whopping 14 inches (36 cm)! It is found in cold, deep waters.

WOODLICE

The 4,000-plus species of woodlouse and pillbug are crustaceans, cousins of sea creatures like shrimp and crabs. Unlike any other crustacean group, they all live on dry land in all sorts of habitats from deserts to mountains. But there's a chink in their armor: because their exoskeleton isn't waterproof, they can quickly dry out unless they find a dark, damp hiding-place—for example, under a plant pot in your backyard.

COMMON WOODLOUSE

ONISCUS ASELLUS

Lifespan: usually 2 years, but may be up to 4
Size: body 0.6 inches (16 mm).

TWO COLORS

Woodlice molt in two stages: first they unshell the back half, then a few days later, the front. That's why you sometimes see two-toned woodlice.

POO!

Woodlice eat their own poop, to recycle nutrients. And instead of peeing, they give off ammonia gas. Phew!

Stalking the Seabed

Attached to the front end of a sea spider are a proboscis (snout), palps and unusual claw-like organs called chelifores. Not all species have the full kit, though.

The sea spider's abdomen is so thin, it has no room for guts, so these are located in the legs! It has no gills either, but takes in oxygen via its exoskeleton.

The long, thin legs are useful for sea spiders that have to wade through seabed muck. Sea spiders in shallower zones tend to have stouter, stronger limbs.

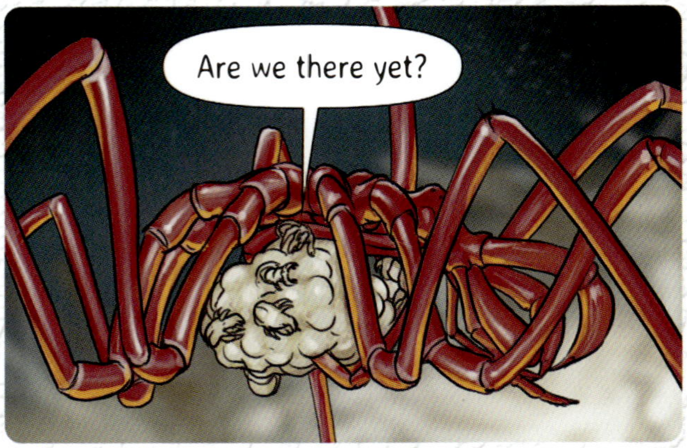

Sea spiders have a pair of ovigers—leg-like limbs that are normally folded up against the body. Both male and female use these to carry eggs and babies.

Most sea spiders are smaller than a mosquito, but in the waters off Antarctica there are giants measuring up to 2 feet (60 cm) across their legspan, and they rub shoulders with monster worms and crustaceans. It's thought that the high oxygen content of cold water helps support these larger-than-normal life forms.

SEA SPIDERS

With their eight legs, the sea spiders may look like land spiders, but they're a wholly unrelated group of ancient marine arthropods. They are found worldwide, from shallow waters to deep ocean trenches. All sea spiders are scavengers or predators, with a long sharp snout for sucking a snack from the bodies of sea anemones and other seabed life. And, with a few exceptions, they're all unbelievably thin!

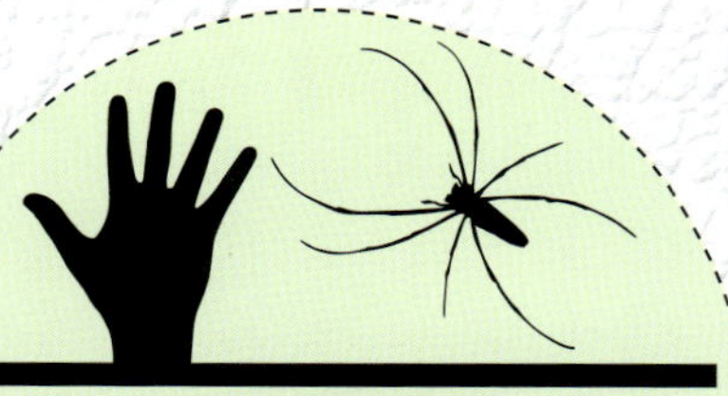

SEA SPIDERS
CLASS: PYCOGONIDA
Lifespan: not known
Size: legspan 0.02–24 in. (0.6 mm–60 cm).

NO BREATHING

A typical sea spider is so skinny, it has no room for lungs or gills, so it doesn't breathe. Instead, the body absorbs oxygen directly from seawater.

TINY MUSCLES

The leg muscles of some sea spiders are microscopically small: they are formed from a single cell.

Skin Crawlers

There are two main types of louse. Some suck blood and other body fluids, and others nibble on skin, feathers, dried blood, and other surface grot.

One bird, the hooded pitohui of New Guinea, has toxic feathers and skin. Scientists think this may be an adaptation for keeping lice away.

Because nits (eggs) and adults cannot survive more than 24 hours away from a host's warmth, the lice use spit to glue their nits to hair or feathers.

There are flies that behave like lice. Louse flies have small (or no) wings, but cling tight to their host—such as a dog or bat—and suck its blood.

During World War I, thousands of soldiers suffered trench fever, a bacterial disease spread by lice that infested their clothing. Symptoms included a fever, headaches, and leg pains. A favorite pastime was squishing the lice in their shirts.

LICE

Almost all mammals have something unpleasant in common. Lice! There are some 5,000 species of these tiny, wingless insects, and all are ectoparasites. They cling tightly to the skin or hair of a host and feed either by sucking its warm blood or chewing bits of dead skin. We humans are host to three species, which lay their nits (eggs) in our hair and on our clothes. Are you itching yet?

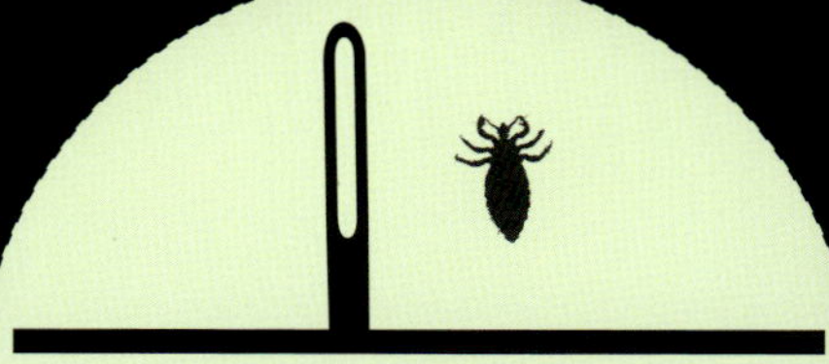

HUMAN HEAD LOUSE

PEDICULUS HUMANUS CAPITIS

Lifespan: 30 days from egg to death

Size: 0.09–0.1 in. (2.5–3 mm).

PARASITES

Bats and whales have no insect lice but do have other parasites of their own. For example, whales have crustacean lice measuring up to 1 inch (2.5 cm) long.

NITS

Lice have probably always plagued humans. When archaeologists opened 3,000-year-old Egyptian tombs, they found nits on mummies.

Champion Jumpers

Ever seen a flea going backwards? Nope. Backward-pointing bristles on its body help it to push constantly—and rapidly—forward.

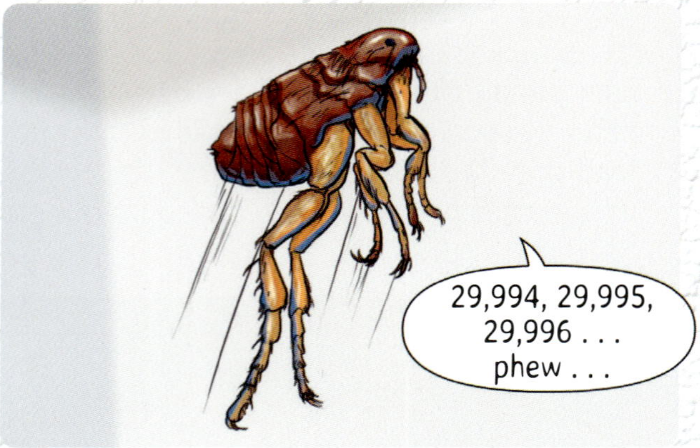

A flea can jump 30,000 times nonstop! It jumps by flexing a pad of resilin (a highly elastic protein), then releasing the energy through its legs.

Flea eggs, laid on the host, hatch into legless larvae, which eat the dried blood in the poop of adult fleas. Eggs and larvae may drop off a host at any time. The larva later pupates (develops inside a pupa), often resting in the carpet for months until a host walks near. Then it suddenly springs out to jump on board.

Fleas breed so fast that, in just three weeks, a single adult pair can populate your pet with a thousand more fleas.

In 1330–1353, a plague known as the Black Death killed more than 75 million people worldwide. The bacterium responsible was carried by fleas on rats.

FLEAS

These little wingless insects, tormentors of your pet cat or dog (or you), are perfectly designed. Powerful hind limbs launch them onto a host, and needle-like mouthparts stab the skin to release a blood meal. Like lice, fleas need their hosts. Hatched adults only live for a few days without feeding, so they snuggle in tight, and their slim, armor-plated bodies are almost impossible to dislodge or crush.

CAT FLEA

CTENOCEPHALIDES FELIS

Lifespan: 1 month or more depending on conditions

Size: 0.03–0.07 in. (1–2 mm).

ANIMAL HOSTS

Rodents, rabbits, hoofed mammals, bats, birds . . . many different animals, along with the carnivores, can be carriers of fleas.

SLIPPERY MOVES

Some fleas are self-lubricating. Pores in the body release an oily material that helps them slip quickly through fur.

Making You Itch

Mites infest animals of all sizes, from elephants to ants. These mites are using their ant host to hitch a ride to somewhere new.

Dust mites love living in our pillows, where they can eat flakes of dead skin. Their poop can cause allergic reactions that make people sneeze and cough.

To get blood from a host, such as a deer, a tick latches onto the body and bites into the skin. As it drinks, its abdomen swells up and darkens. After a female has fed, she drops to the ground and lays her eggs.

A tick can taste with its toes. It does this with an olfactory organ (known as Haller's organ) located in each of its front two feet.

Ticks spread serious diseases. Lyme disease, a bacterial infection that leaves you feeling stiff and tired (sometimes for years), is spread by the deer tick.

MITES AND TICKS

Both these creatures are eight-legged cousins of the spiders. Mites are found all over the world and even in your bed—though you need a microscope to see them. Some eat organic matter (dead or living plants, dandruff, earwax . . .). Others are parasites on plants or on all kinds of animals, including humans. They burrow into the skin, feed on tissue and fluids, and cause misery. Ticks are easier to see—they are basically large mites.

MITE

SUBCLASS: ACARI

Lifespan: usually 1 month

Size: from microscopic up to 0.4 in. (10 mm).

SKIN DISEASE

If you see a homeless dog scratching at rough, bare patches of skin, it's probably suffering from mange—an infection caused by mites.

HUMAN CONTACT

You can pick up ticks yourself from a walk in long grass. They must be removed carefully, so that the head isn't left buried in the skin.

Survival Tricks

In defense, millipedes may coil up into a whorl, protecting the head. The masters at this are the pill millipedes, which look rather like pillbugs (page 52).

Many millipedes deter predators by oozing bad-tasting chemicals. Motyxia species glow, which is thought to be a warning that they contain cyanide.

Meerkats and coatis are mammals that eat millipedes. They roll them on the ground to "detox" them first. And some monkeys rub the chemicals into their coat as a knockout mosquito repellent!

Some soft-bodied millipedes have tufts of barbed bristles, which they wipe off against enemies, such as ants, to tangle them up.

Millipedes have been known to cause train crashes by swarming over railroad tracks. When the wheels squish the millipedes, the trains slip and derail.

MILLIPEDES

These harmless vegetarians feed on decaying matter on the forest floor, ooching along by means of waves that ripple along their many legs. Harmless? Well, not quite. To fend off predators, they can ooze—or, in some cases, squirt—such nasty toxins as hydrogen cyanide, hydrochloric acid, and benzoquinones, which can burn your skin and dye it brown. Handle with care!

MILLIPEDE
CLASS: DIPLOPODA
Lifespan: up to 10 years or more
Size: 0.03–15 in. (2–380 mm).

LEG COUNT

Millipedes are diplopods, with two pairs of legs per body segment. Depending on species, they can have from 24 to 750 legs.

FOSSIL PROOF

Fossils with ozopores—the tiny holes from which millipedes leak their toxins—prove these chemical defenses are at least 420 million years old.

Leggy Hunters

Centipedes like to be in tight spaces: they are happiest when both their upper and lower surfaces are touching something firm.

Centipedes don't mind a bit of cannibalism and will gladly eat other centipedes, especially if they find an injured one that cannot escape.

Some centipedes can raise their forequarters into the air and catch bees or wasps in flight! The Peruvian giant centipede is a 12-inch-long (30-cm) monster that has perfected the art of hanging from cave roofs. Despite having poor eyesight, it can catch bats in flight as they leave their roost in the evening.

Many centipedes are model parents. For example, a mother may lick her eggs to keep them free of fungi, or curl her body protectively around hatchlings.

If caught by the legs, a centipede can drop them. While the wriggling legs distract the attacker, the animal escapes. New legs grow after molting.

CENTIPEDES

Running on up to 360 legs, centipedes are super-fast, fleeing from view if you uncover them in the yard. Sunlight dries them, so they usually spend the day in a moist hiding-place, coming out at night to hunt. Armed with venom-packed pincers, centipedes prey on anything they can catch. Small species hunt flies and beetles; tropical giants may tackle birds, lizards, and mice—and give humans a nasty bite, too.

CENTIPEDE
CLASS: CHILOPODA
Lifespan: up to 10 years
Size: 0.4–12 in. (10–300 mm).

HYGIENE
After feeding, centipedes carefully clean their antennae and legs – all of them!—by running them through their mouthparts.

IN A DASH
The American house centipede can cover 16 in. (40 cm) in a second. That's more than 10 body lengths.

INCREDIBLE JOURNEY

The liver fluke's life cycle begins when an adult, living in a mammal's liver, sheds eggs. These come out in the mammal's droppings, such as a cowpat.

A snail eats some cow poop and, with it, some fluke eggs. The eggs then develop into tiny forms called cercariae, which multiply inside the snail.

Irritated by the cercariae, the snail coughs them up in a slime ball, which is later discovered by an ant. The thirsty ant consumes some slime, and with it, some cercariae. These travel into the ant's brain and control its behaviour, so that it becomes a mindless zombie.

Every evening, the ant climbs a blade of grass and grips the tip with its teeth, then just sits there. Hours later, it returns to its colony but repeats this night after night.

Eventually, a cow chomps the grass stem and swallows the ant with its parasitic cargo. The adult flukes develop and burrow into the cow's liver to lay eggs of their own.

LIVER FLUKE

Flukes are also known as flatworms and belong to a group called the trematodes. They are parasites that enter the guts of snails, fish, and birds, as well as sheep or cattle, where they feast on the host's body fluids. Flukes can make livestock so sick that farmers sometimes lose entire herds. How the flatworms enter those bodies is truly astonishing as it involves not one, but several hosts . . .

LANCET LIVER FLUKE
DICROCOELIUM DENDRITICUM
Lifespan: dependent on host
Size: adult up to 0.6 in. (15 mm).

INFESTATIONS
Humans can suffer from fluke infestations, too. One way to get them is by eating unwashed watercress or undercooked meat.

KILLERS
One group of trematodes, the blood flukes, is responsible for killing up to 200,000 people each year, mostly in Africa, Asia, and South America.

Silk & Orb Webs

Some spiders have a *cribellum*—a rack of extra spinnerets—that spins a fine silk that is then combed by the legs to make "woolly" silk for snaring prey.

Silk is stretchy and strong, and spiders often spin a "dragline" when they leap or drop from a perch—such as a twig—to catch their fall.

Silk is so strong that native peoples in New Guinea once wove it over wooden hoops to make nets for fishing in rivers.

A textile artist in Madagascar collected gold-colored silk from more than one million orb weavers to make a beautiful cape.

Stabilimenta are silken zigzags that some spiders weave into their webs. Do these eye-catching designs help attract insect prey by reflecting ultraviolet light, or do they keep birds away by making the web more visible? Do they help to make the spider look bigger? Experts aren't quite sure.

MAKING SILK

Stored as a liquid, spider silk dries into a thread after being squeezed out of the spinnerets. Spiders can spin different kinds of silk: sticky for trapping prey, non-sticky for walking on, extra-strong for hanging from, and so on. Their most famous creation is the beautiful, spiralling orb web, but many spiders build more messy-looking, three-dimensional tangle webs.

GOLDEN ORB WEB SPIDER

NEPHILA CLAVIPES

Body size: female up to 2 in. (50 mm); male 0.25–0.3 in. (5–8 mm)

Where found: North, Central and South America.

STRONG STUFF

Spider silk is five times stronger than steel of the same thickness. One day, spider silk may be used to make bullet-proof vests for soldiers.

GARDEN SPIDERS

A garden spider may use up to 197 ft (60 m) of silk in a typical orb web but can usually finish the task within an hour.

Tunnels & Trapdoors

A burrowing spider uses spines on its fangs to dig a hole in the soil. It then waterproofs the burrow walls with layers of mud, spit, and silk.

A trapdoor spider adds a hinged door made of silk, mud, and grasses to its burrow. This hides the spider as it sits in wait for prey to wander by.

With its door shut, the burrow is hidden from view. But spider-hunting wasps can usually spot the entrance. The door is no proof against floods, either.

Spiders in the family *Agelenidae*, which build sheet webs above ground, add funnel-like hideaways to their webs, from which they rush out to grab prey.

The trapdoor spider *Cyclosmia* has a flat-ended abdomen covered with a tough plate. It uses this to plug itself inside its burrow if threatened.

WEB TRAPS

Ancient spiders lived in holes in the ground. Some spiders still live like this today, particularly the primitive species known as *mygalomorphs*. Trapdoor spiders often add hinged lids to hide their entrance. Funnel-web spiders, however, ring their entrances with silken "trip wires" that alert them when prey is walking nearby. Above the ground, some spiders add protective tunnels of silk to their webs.

BANDED TUNNEL WEB SPIDER

HEXATHELE HOCHSTETTERI

Body size: up to 0.78 in. (20 mm)

Where found: New Zealand.

SUPER STRONG

Using its barbs and fangs to hold its trapdoor closed, the California trapdoor spider *Bothriocyrtum californicum* can resist a record-breaking pull of up to 38 times its own weight.

MASTER DIGGERS

Trapdoor spiders can dig tunnels 12–15 in. (30–40 cm) deep in the ground and live up to 30 years.

VENOM & HUNTING

Spiders' fangs work in one of two ways. The fangs on mygalomorphs (suborder *Orthognatha*) work up and down together, a bit like a pair of pickaxes . . .

. . .whereas in the so-called "true" spiders (suborder *Labidognatha*), the fangs open and close in a side-to-side pincer action.

Trapdoor spiders are sit-and-wait predators. When prey walks near, they burst out and grab it, then pull it back into their lair.

When an insect blunders into an orb web, it takes only 5–10 seconds for the spider to rush out and bite it. Then it wraps the prey in silk before eating it.

Jumping spiders (family *Salticidae*) pounce on their prey like tigers. There are more than 5,000 species of jumping spider worldwide. Two of their eight eyes, the middle pair, are especially large and look directly forward, helping them judge accurate distances over a range of several inches. (It also makes them look rather cute!)

TOXIC BITE

Almost all spiders rely on venom for hunting: one quick bite and their dinner stops struggling! When a spider stabs its fangs into prey, powerful venom flows out through the hollow fangs and causes paralysis or death, so the spider can feed at leisure. The venom softens the victim's insides into a liquid "soup," which the spider then sucks out. But first, of course, a spider has to catch its prey.

WOLF SPIDER

FAMILY LYCOSIDAE

Body size: 0.4–1.4 in. (10–35 mm)

Where found: Worldwide.

FANGS

The woodlouse spider specializes in eating—can you guess?—woodlice (pill bugs). It has very strong fangs for piercing their exoskeleton.

VENOM

There are two main venom types. Neurotoxins attack the prey's nervous system and stop it moving. Cytotoxins dissolve the guts. Spiders may have one kind or a mixture of both.

THROWING & SPITTING

The net-caster first spins a frame as a support structure. It then spins a small, net-like web onto its hind legs. The net silk is very stretchy.

The spider now hangs downwards from its hind legs and holds the little net in its front four legs. It is ready to pounce.

When a beetle walks into range, the spider stretches the net out by up to ten times its original size, and casts it over the prey. The silk, spun using the spider's cribellum (see page 68), is made up of strands so crinkly and fine that the prey becomes completely entangled in it.

The spitting spider squirts twin jets of silky venom from its fangs. Meanwhile, its body vibrates from side to side to create zigzag patterns in the silk, which glues the prey down like a sticky net. The attack is so fast (about three-hundredths of a second) that it can only be seen with a slow-motion camera.

AMBUSH PREDATORS

Net-casting spiders live in warm habitats from South America to Malaysia and Australia. They spin a little web that is just like a net, wait, then throw it down over a passing victim. They use their superb night vision—twelve times better than ours—to locate prey in darkness. Spitting spiders, which are more or less worldwide, squirt a mix of venom, glue, and silk at their prey to pin it down.

NET-CASTING SPIDER
DEINOPIS RAVIDA
Body size: female up to 0.7 in. (18 mm), male up to approx. 0.5 in. (14 mm)
Where found: Queensland, Australia.

OGRES
Net-casting spiders are also called ogre-faced spiders. Their scientific name, *Deinopis,* means fearsome appearance.

PERFECT AIM
The bolas spiders of Africa, America, and Australasia spin a ball of sticky silk on a line, then swing it at flying moths to knock them out of the air.

BIG EYES
The large pair of eyes on an ogre-faced spider are the biggest simple eyes, relative to body size, of any arthropod.

Fishing

With a film of air around its abdomen allowing it to breathe, the diving bell spider spins a canopy of silk underwater, anchoring it to plant stems.

When the spider dives, a coat of air clings to the hairs on its abdomen. The spider hauls its extra-buoyant body down with the help of silken lines.

The air bubble is held underwater in its silken canopy. Once it reaches a certain volume, the bubble fills itself without further effort from the spider because oxygen naturally filters into it from the water. This artificial gill enables the spider to live underwater like a fish—and to hunt fish!

Dolomedes raft spiders have a coat of short, velvety hairs that repel water and help them float. Their sensitive feet detect the vibrations of moving prey, such as insects or small fish, which they catch at or below the surface. They can briefly dive, too, trapping a film of air around the abdomen.

WATERY HOME

How does an air-breathing creature spend its whole life underwater? The diving bell spider, which lives in ponds and rivers, spins itself a silken dome beneath the surface and fills it with air gathered from above. This oxygen tent becomes a home for the spider, which clambers out to hunt fish and other aquatic life. Raft spiders, too, can hunt on or below the surface, thanks to their amazing ability to "walk on water."

DIVING-BELL SPIDER

ARGYRONETA AQUATICA

Size: 0.3–0.7 in. (8–18 mm)

Where found:

Europe and Asia.

UNDERWATER EGGS

Diving-bell spiders even lay eggs underwater. A few days after hatching, the spiderlings leave the nest to spin their own tiny diving bells.

BIG SPIDERS!

Raft spiders can be big, with leg spans as wide as the palm of your hand. Some have been known to catch goldfish!

Camouflage

Matching its background perfectly, a crab spider is more or less invisible to its prey—insects that visit plants to collect nectar and pollen.

Like a commando in camouflage gear, the lichen spider is colored and patterned just like a lichen-covered tree trunk.

Look very carefully near the tideline on American beaches and you may spot the seashore wolf spider—if you can see through its disguise.

The bird dropping spider—disguised as a splotch of poop—sneakily gives off a scent that moths find delicious. They visit . . . but don't leave!

Some of the most amazing camouflage is seen in tree-dwelling spiders, so they can hide from birds during the day. *Left*: the wrap-around spider (*Dolophones*) is named after the way it flattens itself against a branch. *Center/right*: at rest, twig spiders look just like stumpy little nubs of wood on a branch.

CLEVER CONCEALMENT

Spiders can be surprisingly hard to spot! Since most of them are sit-and-wait hunters, they have evolved very good camouflage. This not only conceals them from prey, improving their chances of catching a meal, but it also helps hide them from predators such as birds. Spider camouflage includes amazing colors and patterns, unusual body shapes, and cryptic (mysterious) behavior.

GOLDENROD CRAB SPIDER

MISUMENA VATIA

Size: female 0.25–0.4 in. (6–9 mm); male 0.12–0.15 in. (3–4 mm)

Where found: All around northern hemisphere.

BLENDING IN

Usually found on yellow or white flowers, the goldenrod crab spider can change color to suit its background.

SLOW CHANGE

It takes the spider about six days to change from yellow to white. Changing back takes four times longer because the spider has to make new yellow pigment.

Mimicry

This *Myrmecium* spider has the usual eight legs, but by waving its long front legs in the air just like antennae, it can trick ants into thinking it's one of them.

A ladybird's bright colors signal to birds that it is foul to eat. So it's no surprise that some spiders—like this *Paraplectana*—mimic the ladybird for protection.

Mimicry can go both ways. On the right is *Coccorchestes*, a jumping spider that mimics a bad-tasting weevil . . . while on the left is *Agelasta*, a longhorn beetle that mimics a crab spider! It's not clear why—but being a copycat must help the beetle in some way.

Ero cambridgei (*left*) is a pirate spider that preys on other spiders. Here, it taps the web of a female *Metellina segmentata* in a particular rhythm, to mimic the courtship signals of her mate. This will trick her into coming closer . . . right into Ero's ambush.

SPIDER TRICKERY

Many spiders have evolved to mimic (look, behave, or even smell like) other creatures—such as ants, beetles, or even other spiders. This trickery can enable the spider to get close to prey without raising the alarm. It can also give protection from predators, such as birds or spider-hunting wasps. For example, by looking like a bad-tasting beetle, a spider is less likely to be eaten.

ANT-MIMIC SPIDER

MYRMARACHNE MAXILLOSA

Size: female 0.25 in. (6–7 mm); male 0.2–0.3 in. (5.5–8 mm)

Where found: Southeast Asia, southern China.

ENEMIES

Stinging and biting ants are dangerous to spiders—especially when there's a gang of them—so by mimicking an ant, a spider can avoid attack.

DISCOVERY

It was English naturalist Henry Walter Bates (1825–1892) who figured out that animals gain protection by mimicking others. He realized this while studying butterflies in the Amazon.

Reproduction

Often the female is much bigger than the male. Just look at this pair of *Nephila* orb weavers. She, after all, will have the job of looking after the kids.

The male *Anyphaena* buzzing spider attracts the attention of a female by vibrating his abdomen noisily. It's a bit like ringing a bell!

To avoid being eaten, the male nursery web spider (*left*) may soothe a female (*right*) by offering her a gift of a chewed-up prey animal.

Some spiders wave their legs at each other in a complex sign language, to make sure they are ready to mate with one another.

Egg sacs may be buried, hidden, abandoned, or guarded carefully, depending on species. Here, a raft spider carries her sac beneath her body, while a bird dropping spider has placed hers on a twig.

FEMALES AND YOUNG

A female spider lays eggs, which hatch into spiderlings. These babies don't have the larval or pupal stages seen in most insects—they are true tiny spiders, and before long they are catching their own prey. Sound easy? First, spiders need to mate, and it can be very dangerous for a male spider to approach a big, hungry female. She may decide to eat him!

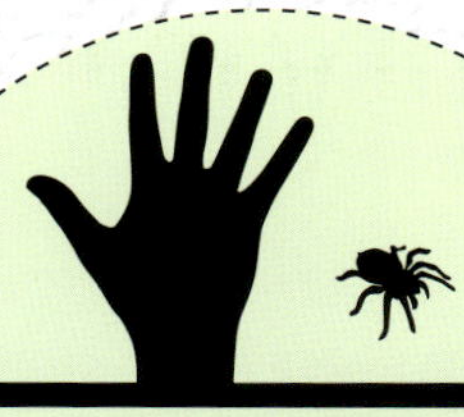

WOLF SPIDER

FAMILY LYCOSIDAE

Body size: 0.4–1.4 in. (10–35 mm)

Where found: Worldwide.

HITCH-HIKERS

The female wolf spider carries her egg sac on her abdomen. When the spiderlings hatch, they climb up onto her back and hitch a ride.

SILKEN TENT

The female nursery web spider makes a tent of silk on a plant in which her babies can grow safely while she stands guard outside.

Spiders & People

The name *tarantula* comes from this spider, *Lycosa tarantula*. Long ago, peasants near Taranto in Italy performed the tarntella dance to cure its bite.

In the 19th century, the black widow (*Latrodectus mactans*)—North America's most venomous spider—often built its web in outhouses

Carefully using a pipette, experts "milk" venom from captive Sydney funnel-web spiders to make medications that can be used to treat spider bites.

Big hairy spiders, like this Mexican red-knee, make popular pets, but overcollection is endangering their populations in the wild.

A single spider can eat about 2,000 insects—flies, mosquitoes, aphids, and so on—in a year. That's why many people put up with spiders in the home and do not squash them. So next time a spider builds its web in your house, give it room, and take a closer look . . .

THE DANGEROUS FEW

The strength of their venom, which can stop prey dead, unfortunately makes a small number of spiders a serious danger to humans. In most species, however, the fangs are just too small to puncture our skin. Also, modern antivenins (medicines) mean that bites are almost never fatal. Nevertheless, you should always treat spiders with respect. Better still, think of them as friends, as they help rid our homes of pests such as flies.

SYDNEY FUNNEL-WEB SPIDER,
ATRAX ROBUSTUS
Body size: 0.6–1.77 in. (15–45 mm)
Where found:
New South Wales, Australia.

BEWARE!
About 12 cm (5 in) across, the Brazilian wandering spider is especially dangerous. It is highly aggressive and injects up to 8 mg of venom—enough to kill about 300 mice.

STRONG BITE
The Sydney funnel-web spider attacks again and again when disturbed. It bites so hard that its fangs can puncture fingernails.

Spiders & Their Enemies

The *Pepsis* tarantula hawk wasp is a huge wasp, up to 2 inches (50 mm) long, with a stinger up to 0.27 inches (7 mm) long. It specializes in hunting spiders.

Having paralysed a spider with its sting, *Pepsis* drags it back to its burrow in the ground. There, it lays a single egg on the spider and covers it over with soil.

When the wasp larva hatches, it eats the spider—beginning with the non-vital organs so that the spider is kept alive for as long as possible.

Mason and potter wasps also gather paralysed spiders for their larvae, storing them in cells built of mud.

The Australasian white-tailed spider (*right*) hunts at night . . . for other spiders. Its favorite prey is *Badumna*, a house spider.

With so many enemies, it's no wonder spiders are shy. Jumping spiders, for instance, often hide in a curled-up leaf by day.

A TOUGH LIFE

Being soft and plump, spiders make a nourishing snack for predators, ranging from birds and lizards to insects and even other spiders. Most fearsome of all are the wasps that sting spiders to paralyze them, then store them to feed to their larvae. There are flies, too, that burrow into a spider and lay eggs. The fly larvae later eat the living spider. The eight-legged life is tough!

BLACK-BACKED KINGFISHER

CEYX ERITHACA

Size: 5 in. (13 cm)

Where found: India, Southeast Asia.

SPIDER HUNTERS

Birds snatch spiders from their webs. They also use the silk as a soft lining for their nests. That's one reason why spiders like to hide during the day.

2D VS 3D

It's thought that, about 130 million years ago, spiders evolved 3D tangle webs from 2D orb webs. The more complex 3D webs were a better defense against wasps.

SIX SPIDER FACTS

The female desert spider *Stegodyphus lineatus* rears just one lot of spiderlings in her life and literally dies for her babies. Her digestive juices soften the food in her stomach, which she then vomits up. Once the spiderlings have eaten that, they devour their mother, leaving just a dry empty husk. Then they leave the nest.

One of the most venomous North American spiders is the brown recluse, or fiddleback, named after the violin-shaped markings on its abdomen. Its bite can kill young children, but luckily, the spider is shy and attacks only reluctantly.

The six-eyed sand spider *Sicarius hahnii*, which lives in desert regions of South Africa, can go 12 months without food or water.

Really big mygalomorph spiders can kill and eat snakes—even 18-inch (45-cm) rattlesnakes. They typically go for the snake behind the head, inflicting a fatal bite.

In parts of Cambodia, especially the town of Skuon, locals serve up crispy-fried spiders, each about as big as your hand. The taste, apparently, is halfway between chicken and fish!

The spiders in one family, the *Uloboridae*, have no venom fangs. Instead, they kill prey by wrapping it in very fuzzy silk—sometimes hundreds of meters of it—which eventually crushes the captive. Then they vomit digestive juices over the victim to soften it into an edible "soup."

FLYING INSECT RECORD-BREAKERS

The largest locust swarm on record covered a 77-square-mile (200-km^2) area of Kenya, Africa, in 1954. It was estimated to contain 10 billion locusts.

What's the world's biggest moth?

That depends on what you're measuring. The Atlas moth (*Attacus atlas*) and hercules moth (*Coscinocera hercules*) have the greatest wing area but not the widest wingspan. That award probably goes to the white witch (above) (*Thysania agrippina*), an American species spanning up to 11.3 inches (289 mm).

The painted lady (*Vanessa cardui*) is not only one of the world's most widespread butterflies, but its populations also make an epic migration each year. In spring, as their southern habitat heats up, they head north as far as the Arctic. Then in fall, as northern temperatures cool, they head south again, completing a round trip of up to 9,300 miles (15,000 km). But no butterfly ever makes the full trip. Instead, the migrant swarms go through several generations on each leg. In human terms, it would be like setting off for your annual vacation, but dying on the way, with your children's children's children finally arriving at the resort.

The world's toughest moth is possibly the Arctic woolly bear (*Gynaephora groenlandica*), which lives in the polar north. Its life cycle from egg to adult takes around seven years . . . partly because the shaggy caterpillar spends more than 10 months of the year frozen, which leaves very little time for feeding! Uniquely among insects, the caterpillar can survive temperatures below -76°F (-60°C), but to do so it must pack its body with natural antifreeze chemicals before winter kicks in.

Amazing Insect Feats

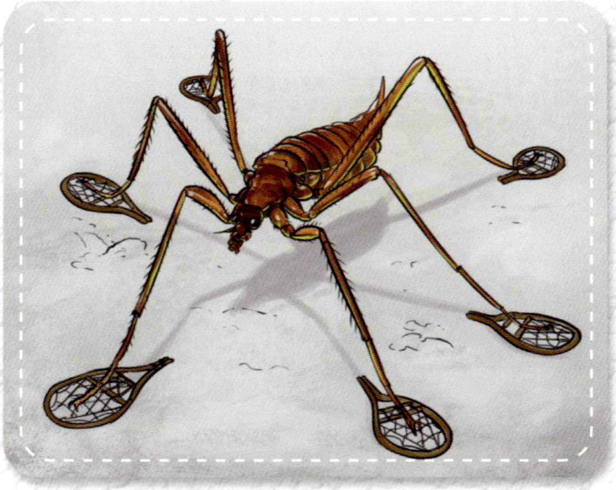

What do you call a fly with no wings?

A walk! Actually, there are lots of wingless flies. They include the snow flies in the genus *Chionea*, which—as their name suggests—can be found in winter, walking on snow. Their haemolymph (blood) contains a natural antifreeze. Other wingless examples include bat flies—true flies that live as parasites on the fur of batsand can only take flight by hitching a ride.

Can insect poisons save human lives?

Scientists are studying several insect poisons for use in anti-cancer drugs. These poisons include pederin (see page 25), as well as DHMA, a rare fatty acid found in soldier beetles. Another is MP1, a toxin from the venom of a Brazilian wasp, which seems to kill cancer cells while leaving normal cells unharmed.

How many ants are there?

At any one time, there are about a quadrillion of them—1,000,000,000,000,000—on Earth.

Can goats rescue insects?

Introduced rats, stoats, and other predators killed so many giant weta in New Zealand that the insects were believed extinct on the mainland. Then in 1962, giant weta were discovered in a clump of spiky gorse bushes near Mahoenui in the North Island. They had survived because the grazing of goats had kept the gorse growth so dense that rats couldn't penetrate it. More than 50 years on, the weta are still there.

Parasites on Parade

Many mini beasts are parasites—creatures that depend on other creatures for their survival—perhaps to gain free food or shelter. Below are a couple more parasites you may find interesting . . .

Leeches

Leeches are segmented worms with a sucker at each end of a muscular, stretchy body. With around 680 species known worldwide, they range from 0.3 to 12 inches (7 to 300 mm). Most live in sluggish fresh water, where they latch onto almost any creature—living or dead—to suck its fluids. They often go for snails, but if you're unlucky, a leech may find you. If you don't remove it first, it'll drop off after drinking its fill of blood.

When biting, leeches inject a chemical—hirudin—that prevents blood clotting, so wounds can leak for hours after the leech has been removed. For more than 2,000 years, drawing blood was a common cure for a wide range of ailments, and doctors put leeches on their patients to do the blood-letting. Some still do!

Tapeworms

Tapeworms belong to a group called the platyhelminthes (meaning flatworms). One type commonly found in humans is *Diphyllobothrium*, which you can pick up by eating raw or undercooked fish infested with the tapeworm larvae. The tapeworm then grows in your gut, where it feeds by absorbing nutrients. In other words, it eats your food. Tapeworms don't really qualify as minibeasts, given that they can rapidly grow to terrifying lengths. One of the longest ever found in a human gut was 82 feet (25 m) long! But don't worry: you can usually get rid of them with tablets.

INDEX

The Author

British-born Matt Turner graduated from Loughborough College of Art in the 1980s. Since then he has worked as a picture researcher, editor, and writer. He has authored books on diverse topics including natural history, earth sciences, and railways, as well as hundreds of articles for encyclopedias and partworks, covering everything from elephants to abstract art. He and his family currently live in Auckland, Aotearoa/New Zealand, where he volunteers for the local coast guard unit and dabbles in painting.

The Artist

Born in Medellín, Colombia, Santiago Calle is an illustrator and animator trained at Edinburgh College of Art in the UK. He began his career as a teacher, which led him to deepen his studies in sequential art. Santiago founded his art studio Liberum Donum in Bogotá in 2006, partnering with his brother Juan. Since then, they have dedicated themselves to producing concept art, illustration, comic strip art, and animation.

Picture Credits (abbreviations: t = top; b = bottom; c = center; l = left; r = right)

© www.shutterstock.com: 1 c, 2 cl, 4 c, 6 tc, 6 br, 7 tc, 7 bl, 9 c, 11 c, 13 c, 15 c, 19 c, 21 c, 23 c, 25 c, 27 c, 29 c, 31 c, 33 c, 35 c, 37 c, 39 c, 43 c, 45 c, 47 c,.49 c, 51 c, 53 c, 55 c, 59 c, 61 c, 63 c, 65 c, 67 c, . 69 c, 73 c, 75 c, 77 c, 79 c, 81 c, 83 c, 85 c, 87 c.

11 c By Dinobass (own work) [CC BY-SA 4.0 (http://creativecommons.org/licenses/by-sa/4.0)] via Wikimedia Commons. 13 c Joseph Berger/© Bugwood.org/CC-BY-3.0-US. 41 © Richard Bartz, Munich (Wiki Commons). 57 c © CDC/ Frank Collins, Ph.D / James Gathany. 71 c © Bryce MQuillan NZ

Every effort has been made to trace the copyright holders, and we apologise in advance for any uninterntional omissions. We would be pleased to insert the appropriate acknowldgement in any subsequent edition of this publication.